Things That
Make You Go

YUCK!

Rare marsh grasshopper

Things That Make You Go YUCK!

Crooked Critters

Jenn Dlugos & Charlie Hatton

Prufrock Press Inc.
Waco, Texas

Library of Congress Cataloging-in-Publication Data

Names: Dlugos, Jenn, author.|Hatton, Charlie, author.
Title: Things that make you go yuck! : crooked critters/
  by Jenn Dlugos and Charlie Hatton ; edited by Lacy Compton.
Other titles: Crooked critters
Description: Waco, Texas : Prufrock Press Inc., [2017]|
  Audience: Ages 9-12. |Includes bibliographical references.
Identifiers: LCCN 2016032220|ISBN 9781618216090 (pbk.)
Subjects: LCSH: Animals--Adaptation--Juvenile literature.|Adaptation
  (Biology)--Juvenile literature.|Animals--Miscellanea--Juvenile
  literature.
Classification: LCC QH546 .D58 2017 | DDC 578.4--dc23
LC record available at https://lccn.loc.gov/2016032220

Copyright © 2017, Prufrock Press Inc.
Edited by Lacy Compton
Cover and layout design by Raquel Trevino

ISBN-13: 978-1-61821-609-0

Printed in the United States of America.

At the time of this book's publication, all facts and figures cited are
the most current available. The author and Prufrock Press Inc. make
no warranty or guarantee concerning the information and materials
given out by organizations or content found at websites, and we
are not responsible for any changes that occur after this book's
publication. If you find an error, please contact Prufrock Press Inc.

Prufrock Press Inc.
P.O. Box 8813
Waco, TX 76714-8813
Phone: (800) 998-2208
Fax: (800) 240-0333
http://www.prufrock.com

Red ant

Table
of Contents

Peregrine falcon

Introduction

Bullying. Burglary. Rioting. Fraud. That may sound like a list of offenses committed by some scary characters in your school's detention hall, but it's actually the sort of behavior that the animals, plants, and microscopic critters around us engage in every day. For many, their very survival—and the survival of their species—may depend on it.

The Drive to Survive

We like to think of the creatures in nature getting along, cooperating, living together in peace and harmony without fighting or trampling or eating each other.

(Except for vegetables. Pretty much everything eats them. Even vegetarians.)

But often, nature isn't quite so "nice." Surviving in the wild is a lot of work—and if an organism can save energy by taking advantage of a situation (or a neighbor), then it usually will. That could mean anything from invading someone's home, to impersonating a potential mate, to full-out mind control. Seriously, the villains in superhero comics have nothing on some of the creatures in our own backyards.

But why do they do such dastardly things to each other? The answer starts with resources.

Use the Resource Force

All species use available natural resources, whether that's food, water, shelter, or territory. But there aren't always enough resources to go around, which puts individuals in direct competition with each other. The stakes are high—survival is on the line—and organisms try any method they can to stay alive.

A successful method is called an *adaptation*. It helps the organism survive in its environment, allowing it to find resources, protect itself, or successfully reproduce. Over time, the species as a whole may come to depend on that adaptation for survival. Which is great for the species—it may even mean the difference between survival and extinction. But it's not always so good for other species nearby.

Rowdy Neighbors

Adaptations usually affect more than the species that develop them. It could be an extreme effect—if some other species is surviving by eating you, for instance, you'll probably notice that pretty quickly. Other adaptations steal directly from neighboring species, by tricking or sneaking or bullying resources out of them. And some steal indirectly—if a species grows large enough in size or number, it can suck up all of the free resources before anyone else.

Competing species nearby will have to move elsewhere, adapt themselves—or pay the price. Nature is a constant game of individuals and species trying to one-up the other, in a never-ending race for limited precious resources. (And also, sometimes, vegetables.)

Neither Naughty nor Nice

Unlike many detention hall hooligans, these "crooked" critters don't act up out of boredom or spite. If they steal and cheat and bully—and, oh boy, do they ever—it's simply because they have to. They're born into situations where they have to walk all over other species (sometimes literally) just to see another day. A day when some other species will probably walk all over them, too. It's not always "nice," exactly. But that's nature.

Red fox

1 Big Bad Bullies

Nobody likes a bully. Pushy pests who tease and torment, harass and harry, and pick on the little guys and girls—bullies are no fun to be around. But if you think humans have the bully market cornered, think again. In this chapter, you'll meet species that make most bullies look like babies.

Take the Crooked Critters Quiz!

This bully is so notorious, William Shakespeare used it in the title of one of his plays.

a. Fox   b. Shrew   c. Weasel

Find out the answer at the end of the chapter!

Tale of the Tape(worm)

Some prefer cool weather; others like it hot. The three-spined stickleback is a species of fish that lives in coastal waters, and it's firmly in the "cool" camp. Sticklebacks usually like to swim in water around 60 degrees Fahrenheit or 16 degrees Celsius. That's cold enough to make you shiver in your swimsuit, but sticklebacks don't seem to mind—unless they have company.

Some sticklebacks play host, against their will, to the parasitic tapeworm species *Schistocephalus solidus* (shiss-toe-CEFF-uh-luss sah-LID-us). This worm grows in the intestines of animals, and has a complicated life cycle. The tapeworm can only mature into an adult and lay eggs in the gut of a bird, but spends most of its life inside a stickleback. So how does it get from the fish to a fowl?

By bullying the fish, from the inside. Tapeworms affect the sticklebacks' appearance, bloating some infected fish to twice their normal size. But the worms also modify behavior. Sticklebacks with tapeworms are more likely to swim alone, less likely to flee predators, and tend to seek out warmer waters, which makes the worms grow faster. None of this makes the fish happy, but it makes it more likely to be eaten by a bird, which is what the worms were after all along. Talk about "thinking with your stomach."

A Worm's Life

The full life cycle of an *S. solidus* worm looks like this: an egg is laid in the intestine of an infected bird, and drops (hitchhiking in bird poop) into water. It hatches and infects a tiny crustacean called a *copepod* (KOH-puh-pod). That's eaten by a stickleback, while the worm inside the fish gets eaten by a bird. The tapeworm grows in the bird's intestines, lays eggs, and the cycle starts anew.

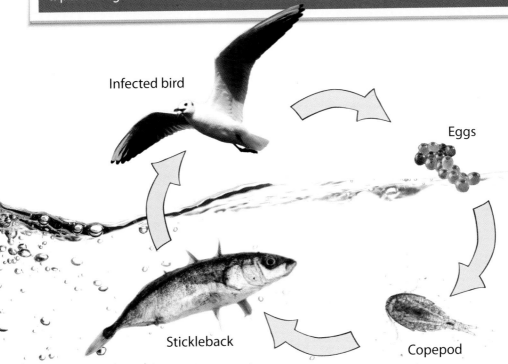

Infected bird

Eggs

Stickleback

Copepod

Zombie Ants
Come Out at Night

Lancet liver flukes are members of a species of tiny flatworm, and they have pretty rough childhoods. Each fluke starts as an egg in the gut of a cow or sheep, and gets pooped out into a field. The egg is eaten by a snail, where the fluke grows until the snail spits it out in a ball of slime. And little orphan Annie thought she had a hard knock life.

The slimy young flukes are eaten by ants, where things get really interesting. The flukes need to get eaten by another large animal to reproduce. So the lancet liver fluke makes the ants into zombies. But only at night, because everyone knows that's the best time for zombies.

While most flukes eaten by an ant travel to the abdomen, one or two invade the nervous system. There, the flukes can control the ant's behavior after dark. At night, ants usually return to their nests, but fluke-infested "zombie" ants do not. Instead, the flukes force the ants to climb a tall blade of grass and chomp down with their mandibles (jaws).

The ants stay there all night, clenched tight onto a plant. The flukes' goal is to get the ant accidentally eaten by a grazing animal—that's why they drive the ants high onto grass and have them hold on tight. But once the sun is up, the flukes release control. Otherwise, the ants would die in the heat and let go, which is no help to anyone. So the ants go about their day normally—until nighttime arrives, and the zombie flukes take over their brains again.

No Flukes Is Good Flukes

The lancet liver fluke causes a disease called *dicrocoeliasis* (die-crow-COLE-ee-ay-sis) in cows and sheep. The infection can cause slower growth, reduced milk production, and liver damage or failure. Though humans can be infected, cases are rare and usually not severe.

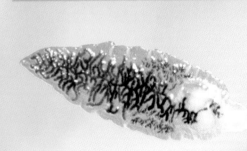
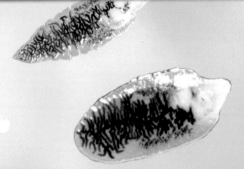

A Snail's Worst Nightmare

Infected tentacle

Healthy tentacle

If a "green-banded broodsac" sounds like a monster from a late-night horror movie . . . well, that's actually not far from the truth. Especially if you happen to be a snail.

The green-banded broodsac is a species of flatworm that breeds in the digestive tracts of birds, and whose eggs are excreted among the birds' droppings onto the ground. There, the worms need a snail to continue their life cycle, but woe to the unsuspecting snails who "help."

Once eaten by a snail, green-banded broodsac larvae live up to their horrifying name. The larvae develop into a form called a *sporocyst* (SPORE-oh-sist), which grows

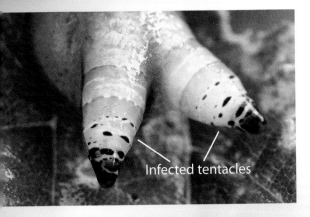

Infected tentacles

into a long tube inside one of the snail's tentacles. The sporocyst can contain dozens or hundreds of young, and swells the tentacle into a fat structure with green stripes and a colored tip. What's more, the young inside the sac move in response to light, making the tentacle pulse and throb in rhythm.

This is all an attempt to get the snail eaten by a bird, where the worms can lay new eggs. The throbbing banded tentacles are thought to resemble caterpillars or grubs—two of birds' favorite snacks. Taking over the snails' tentacles may also make them less sensitive to light. Although most snails shun bright sunlight, infected snails stay out in the open longer and move around more, which makes them—or at least their tentacles—likelier to end up as bird brunch.

Keep Left

Scientists aren't sure why, but green-banded broodsacs seem to prefer snails' left tentacles. If multiple worms infect the same snail—or the snail has lost its left tentacle, perhaps from an earlier infection—then the right tentacle may be affected, too. But given the option, these flatworms tend to turn left. Maybe they're NASCAR fans.

11

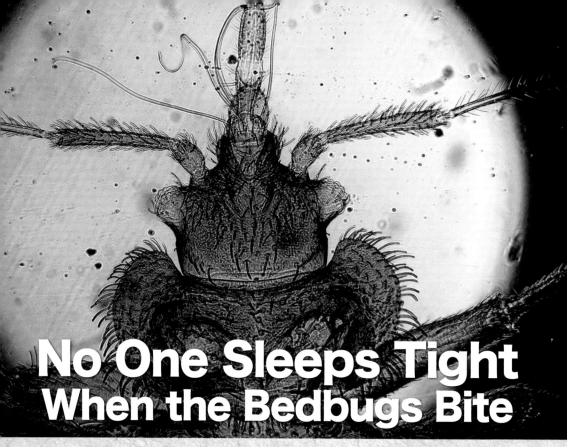

No One Sleeps Tight
When the Bedbugs Bite

Bullies are known for being big and bad, but one of humankind's Most Wanted Bullies is the tiny bedbug, which is barely the size of an apple seed. Bedbugs have been pestering humans for nearly our entire existence, and they are even mentioned in ancient Egyptian writings. They feed on our blood, and they are most active at night, usually biting us when we are fast asleep.

Bedbugs likely originated in caves where they fed on bats. Early humans took shelter in these caves, and these tiny bugs quickly learned just how yummy we are. Bedbugs will bite dogs, cats, birds, and rats, but humans are their preferred snack. A single bedbug can drink six times its weight in blood and leave you with red, itchy welts in the morning. Even if you are awake when the bite occurs, you probably won't feel it—their mouths are equipped with an anesthetic that numbs the skin, keeping us from feeling the bite.

Female bedbugs can lay 250 to 500 eggs in their lifetimes, so if they do crawl into a home, hotel, or dorm room, they spread like wildfire. They are immune to most over-the-counter pesticides, but a pest-fighting professional can rid your home of these pesky buggers, so you can once again sleep tight, without letting these bully bugs bite.

Tight Night?

There is some debate about the exact meaning of "sleep tight" in the phrase "sleep tight, don't let the bedbugs bite." Some believe it dates back to the days when ropes that held up mattresses had to be pulled tight before bed. Others believe it refers to nightshirts and gowns—pull them tight or the bed bugs will creep in. It is very possible that it has no special meaning, since the word "tight" was once commonly used to mean "well."

13

Pucker Up Under the **Parasite**

Ah, December. Holiday shoppers swarm the malls, everyone spreads around the holly jolly, and young lovers snuggle up to kiss under a parasite. We deck our halls with mistletoe in hopes of getting a seasonal smooch, but these festive plants are actually some of the most notorious bullies in the forest.

Most mistletoe species are considered parasites, because they suck food and nutrients from the trees they live on. It's not like they can't make their own food—since they are plants, they can photosynthesize—they simply prefer to be like that friend who's

Heavy load of mistletoe
on an apple tree

always raiding your fridge when he visits. As they grow, mistletoes can kill the tree or shrub they grow on, or at very least, stunt its growth.

The dwarf mistletoe is one parasitic plant that takes bullying to a whole new level. Most mistletoes rely on wind, insects, or small animals to spread their seeds, but dwarf mistletoes grow sticky seeds inside high-pressure shells. When the shell bursts open, seeds shoot out like a rocket at 90 miles an hour, catapulting the seeds into other trees and shrubs. Apparently it's not enough to swipe food from their tree hosts; dwarf mistletoes have to spew spitballs at them, too.

The First Kiss

The first documented incident of kissing under the mistletoe dates back to the 1500s, but no one knows exactly where the holiday tradition started. Our fascination with mistletoes long predates the holiday tradition, however. Some ancient European cultures believed that oak trees were gifts from heaven and the mistletoe growing on them housed the tree's life force in the winter, after the tree lost its leaves.

Treeshrew

Crooked Critters Quiz Answer

This bully is so notorious, William Shakespeare used it in the title of one of his plays.

   a. Fox

   b. Shrew (correct)

   c. Weasel

In Shakespeare's day, "shrew" was an unflattering name given to an aggressive or outspoken woman, which inspired one of his most famous comedies, *The Taming of the Shrew*. Shrews are tiny mammals that have a fierce hunting style. A few species are venomous, and when they do capture their prey, they sometimes pee on it so they can find their meal later by its scent. (We imagine there is not much lunch swapping in the shrew school cafeteria. Yeesh.)

Think About It

Life in the wild is a bit like a sports game with an offense and a defense. The offense tries to steal points from the opposing team. The defense protects its turf. If you made a sports team with your favorite animals, who would be the offense and who be the defense? What special skills does each animal have that will help them against the opposing team? Use any sport you want, or even make up your own!

Carolina locust

2 Mobsters

One rogue organism can cause plenty of mayhem, all by its lonesome. But what happens when they gang up together—to hunt, to invade, or just to crowd together in ridiculous numbers? Then you've got a mob on your hands. Or a flock, or a gang, a gaggle, a herd, or a swarm. And that could cause a whole big bunch of problems.

Take the Crooked Critters Quiz!

These insects have a predictable 17-year life cycle. They live most of their lives underground, emerging at the end of their life cycles all at once to reproduce.

a. Cicadas   b. Locusts   c. Red ants

Find out the answer at the end of the chapter!

Blooms of Doom

Asingle jellyfish can be a problem. It's squishy, slippery, and if you're not careful, you might get stung. Jellyfish use sharp barbs on their tentacles to inject toxins into animals they brush past, whether those animals are potential threats, possible food, or innocent by-swimmers. Some jellyfish toxins are strong enough to seriously injure or kill humans. So even one jellyfish is nothing to sneeze at. Or swim toward. But what about a billion jellyfish? Or more?

One Good Mob Deserves Another

Some jellyfish blooms may owe a tip of the hat—or tentacle—to another "mobbing" occurrence: algae blooms. When ocean algae grow in large numbers, the surrounding area is deprived of oxygen. Fish and other jellyfish competitors can't survive these conditions, but jellyfish can—so algae blooms may indirectly help jellyfish to bloom in huge numbers.

Under certain conditions, local populations of jellyfish can surge to huge numbers, creating masses known as *jellyfish blooms*. These blooms may contain billions of individuals, and can occur all over the world. Although jellyfish generally prefer warmer water, blooms have "blossomed" in recent years near Scotland, Japan, Sweden, China, Australia, and the United States, among other areas. Some blooms spread for 1,000 miles or more and can be seen from space.

That's no good for swimmers, but it's bad news for other reasons, too. Jellyfish blooms disrupt fishing boats, driving away fish and clogging nets. Blooms have also washed through commercial fish farms, killing more than 100,000 fish. And the sheer mass of jellyfish can clog seawater intakes for structures that need them, like coastal power plants and ships—and once, the aircraft carrier *USS Ronald Reagan*. A battleship disabled by jellyfish—now, that's got to sting.

The War on Christmas Island

A battle has raged for years on the remote Christmas Island. It sounds like the plot of an animated holiday special, but it's real—with no elves or Grinches or frosty snowmen involved.

Christmas Island is an isolated Australian territory, hundreds of miles off the mainland in the Indian Ocean. Only about 2,000 people live there, but the island is home to many millions of red crabs. Christmas Island red crabs are famous for their annual migration at the start of the rainy season, usually in October or November—just in time for Christmas. The crabs march from the central rainforest to the shore, where they mate and females release eggs into the sea.

A Christmas Gift for Crabs?

Hope for the Christmas Island crabs may come from an odd ally: a wasp. Scientists at an Australian university hope that introducing a parasitic microwasp species from Malaysia can control the yellow crazy ant population. The wasp attacks an insect that provides the main food source for the ants. By reducing that insect's numbers, they hope the ants' numbers will dwindle, and the crabs (and the island's entire ecosystem) will soon be better off.

But a visitor to Christmas Island has caused huge problems for the crabs. Decades ago, an insect species known as the yellow crazy ant was accidentally brought to the island, probably on imported timber. By the mid-1990s, these ants began to form "supercolonies"—millions of individuals with multiple queens and nests, covering wide areas. The Christmas Island red crabs and yellow crazy ants compete—and lately, the ants have been winning. The ants spray acid as a defense, which has killed tens of millions of crabs over the past 20 years, disrupted migrations, and upset the delicate and unique ecosystem of this remote tropical island.

Wolves in Whales' Clothing

Orcas, also known as killer whales, are fearsome ocean predators. An orca has razor-sharp teeth as long as your finger, can reach 30 feet and 10 tons in size, and swim as fast as 30 miles an hour. But if you think one orca sounds scary, just wait until they get together. On top of their physical skills, orcas are social animals and often hunt in packs. (Or technically, *pods*, the term for a group of whales.) That's why they're sometimes called the "wolves of the sea." Unlike actual wolves, who don't usually enjoy swimming or long ocean cruises.

The scary thing about orcas is that they cooperate in different ways—bad news for sea animals the orcas call "food." Near Antarctica, for instance, orcas hunt seals by making waves. A seal may feel safe on a floating patch of ice—until a pod of orcas rush toward it at once, making a huge wave. The wave washes over the ice, the seal falls off, and the orcas get lunch.

Other times, orcas work like shepherds. Several will circle around schools of small fish, blowing bubbles from below to drive them together and up to the surface. Then the orcas slap the water with their tails, stunning the fish for an easy meal. These cooperative killers don't stop at small prey, though. Orca pods have been observed hunting gray whales much larger than themselves, ambushing dolphins, and cornering narwhals in a shallow-water trap. Orcas are so good at hunting together that maybe we should be calling wolves the "killer whales of the land."

Kings (and Queens) of the Sea

Orcas are found in every ocean on Earth, and can live to be 90 years or older—though those in captivity don't survive as long. Orcas are "apex predators," meaning there's no other species that hunts them. In other words, they're at the top—or the apex—of their food chain.

25

Diaea ergandros

Eight-Legged Social Butterflies

S piders are not exactly chummy critters. Most are chronic "party-of-ones," living in complete solitude until the male meets the female for mating. When this happens, it's anything but a "meet cute." Female black widows get a bad rap for eating their mate, but that doesn't happen all the time, and they are far from the only spiders that do. Even female tarantulas have on occasion eaten their mate before or after mating.

Oddly, some spiders do play nice with each other. *Anelosimus eximius* (pronounced Ah-nehl-AH-si-mus ek-SI-mi-us) are cobweb spiders that spin massive 20-foot webs, which house thousands of spiders. (Imagine walking into *that* spider web. We'll wait here until your body shivers pass.) Most spiders in the colony are females that work together to repair the web and tend to the colony's offspring. Just like birds, they regurgitate food to feed the babies. (We can almost hear the spider kids whining, "Mom! Not spider barf for dinner again!" from here.)

Socializing with spiders can be risky business, and one particular type of social crab spider actually eats its own mother. The mom spider fetches food for her babies, but if there isn't enough food available, the babies eat her instead. They start by nibbling on her legs. Then they gnaw on her eyes. Finally, they eat her whole. Scientists think the mom's sacrifice teaches the babies not to eat each other, so they can live together in a social community. Either way, this is one mom that definitely says to her kids, "I hope you grow up and have kids just like you."

Anelosimus eximius

Not Exactly Party Animals

Social spiders are definitely the oddballs of the spider world. Out of more than 40,000 species of spiders, only a few dozen species are known to live together in social communities.

We're Not Gonna Need a Bigger Goat(fish)

Yellow saddle goatfish don't look like criminal masterminds, but don't let their cheery yellow bodies and cute googly eyes fool you. They are some of the fiercest predators this side of Jaws, and the complexity of their hunting style makes them a one-of-a-kind fish.

There are many different types of goatfish, and most are solitary hunters. Goatfish hunt for small fish, crabs, and worms using barbels, goatee-like "whiskers" on their chins that help them detect prey. When hunting, they drag their barbels along the sea bottom, rousting up yummy sea critters. We're guessing goatfish parents have no problem getting their children up for school.

(Because fish swim in schools. See what we did there?

All right, stop your groaning. Moving on.)

Yellow saddle goatfish live in coral reefs, which are undersea obstacle courses. It's easy for prey to hide, dodge, and weave in and around the coral, so the yellow saddle goatfish often hunt in teams, with each fish assuming a different role. One fish is the chaser, staying hot on the prey's tail, while the other fish are blockers, standing watch at different exits. The complexity of this coordinated attack is seen in higher vertebrates like wolves, but not often in fish. Some scientists compare their pack hunting skills to lions, which definitely make these goatfish the pride of the sea. (Last bad pun of the chapter. Promise.)

Are Beards in This Season?

Goatfish barbels have taste buds and receptors that pick up chemical signals left by prey. When they're not feeding, goatfish fold up their barbels, switching between the clean-shaven and the bearded look with ease. Very fashion forward of you, goatfish.

New Forest cicada

Crooked Critters Quiz Answer

These insects have a predictable 17-year life cycle. They live most of their lives underground, emerging at the end of their life cycles all at once to reproduce.

a. **Cicadas (correct)**
b. Locusts
c. Red ants

Periodical cicadas are species have life cycles that last either 13 or 17 years, the longest lives of any North American insect. They live most of their lives underground, emerging at the end of their life cycle to reproduce and lay eggs. They are sometimes called "Seventeen Year Locusts," but this is inaccurate. Locusts are not cicadas; they are a type of grasshopper.

Think About It

Filmmakers often use animals or plants in movies to convey certain emotions. A swarm of insects in a horror movie gives you goosebumps, but geese flying in a V formation across the sky may make a scene seem calm or peaceful. Why do you think humans associate some groups of animals with pleasant emotions and others with fear or disgust? If you wrote a movie scene about your favorite animal, what would it be about? What type of emotions would people have watching it?

Musca albina

3 Breaking and Entering

Most humans know that stealing is wrong, but the rules are a bit different in the wild. Some critters' survival is based on snatching, grabbing, and pilfering from other species. This chapter features some of the most cunning and daring burglars in the land and sea.

Take the Crooked Critters Quiz!

Musca albina is a species of fly known for this yucky habit:

a. Drinking sweat from horses for nutrients

b. Building nests out of shed human skin cells

c. Laying eggs in poop balls rolled by beetles

Find out the answer at the end of the chapter!

Bite Your Tongue!

S ome animals really need a lesson in personal space. Parasites are the worst offenders. They survive by mooching off another organism, and the host gets no perks from the deal. By far the biggest personal space violator is a tiny parasite that slowly sucks blood from a fish's tongue until its tongue falls off.

Cymothoa exigua (Sigh-moe-THO-ah ex-ZIG-you-wah) is also called the tongue-eating louse, but this is a misnomer. Lice—the critters that like to curl up in your luscious locks—are insects, while *Cymothoa exigua* are crustaceans, just like lobsters and crabs. These tiny critters sneak into the fish through its gills and attach to the blood supply in its tongue. Without blood, the tongue eventually dies away, but the crustacean attaches itself to the stalk that remains. Oddly, the fish uses the bitey bugger as its replacement tongue, a relationship that can last for the rest of the fish's life. And *Cymothoa exigua* certainly doesn't mind, because it gets a few nibbles of everything the fish eats—a win-win for the tongue-eater (not so much of a win for the recently tongueless fish).

An Unexpected Appetizer

In 2005, someone in the United Kingdom bought a red snapper from a fish market and found one of these creepy crustaceans attached to its tongue, making it the first time these tongue-eating parasites were found on fish sold in the UK. *Cymothoa exigua* are mostly found in the Pacific Ocean between California and the northern part of South America. It's unclear if the crustaceans' range is spreading or it was an isolated incident.

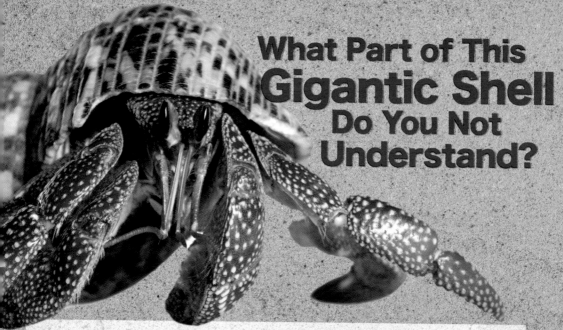

What Part of This Gigantic Shell Do You Not Understand?

Hermit crabs clearly don't want to be bothered. After all, they carry their homes on their backs, which takes the "personal space" thing to new level. Yet, some critters did not get the No Trespassing memo, so even the shy little hermit crab deals with some dastardly home invaders.

Despite their name, many hermit crabs are quite social, forming communal relationships with each other and beneficial relationships with other species. But some critters take the crabs' hospitality a bit too far. Mites are pesky little arachnids well-known by pet owners for their love of chewing on Fido or Fluffy. Some mites also live off hermit crabs, attaching to their legs, eyes, and mouthparts so they can suck the crab's hemolymph (a.k.a. crab "blood"). In severe cases, a crab can lose a limb or even die from a mite infestation.

Master Shell Builder

Hermit crabs live in old snail shells, which they swap out for bigger shells as they grow. If there are no shells available, the crabs can get pretty creative. In Puerto Rico, a hermit crab was found using a large Lego-like toy block as a shell. The crab seemed healthy, but now there is yet another kid in the world screaming, "Where did that piece go? I just had it!"

Some worms actually move right into the crab's shell, poking their head out when the crab eats and snatching food right out of its mouth. As bad as that sounds, there is an even worse invader. One parasitic crustacean attaches to the crab's abdomen to suck its hemolymph. It can cause so much damage that the crab becomes sterile, unable to reproduce.

Maybe we should get the crabs little Keep Out signs to hold in their claws. Perhaps then those pesky invaders will get the message.

Skua

The Taming of the Skua

If all the crooked critters in the book were put on trial for their crimes against other species, a few might get off on a technicality. The skua bird is not one of them. These feathered felons are so good at pillaging and looting that they are also called *avian pirates* or *pirate birds*.

Skua is a name given to several species of seabirds, many which are kleptoparasites (klepto means "to steal"). Skuas snatch food from other birds—sometimes birds much larger than them—using a variety of tactics. They can be stealthy, diving down and stealing unattended morsels before the victims even know what hit them. Sometimes

38

Papua penguin

Phony Baloney

Larger birds like hawks eat skuas and their offspring, but the skuas certainly don't make it easy. They often lure hungry birds away from their nests by faking an injury. The predator, thinking it found itself an easy meal, follows the "injured" bird until the skua flies into the air, simultaneously avoiding capture and saving its eggs.

they even drop down on a bird in midflight, forcing it to drop its catch. If that doesn't work, skuas have a particularly persuasive—and downright terrifying—tactic for getting their grub. They'll snatch a bird and shake it until it regurgitates (in not-so-nice terms, vomits) its recent catch.

Being career crooks, skuas get very aggressive when someone sneaks into their space, especially their breeding grounds. They will dive-bomb anyone who approaches their nests—including people. At least they probably won't shake us until we puke. Unless, of course, we just ate a fish dinner. Then all bets are off.

More Cuckoo / Than Cuckoos

Y ou may have heard about cuckoos, which are pretty rude birds. Not because
they jump out of clocks—though that does seem rude—but because cuckoos
are obligate brood parasites. A brood parasite is a species that uses other
unsuspecting species to raise its young, and "obligate" means they do it all
the time. Cuckoos' only strategy for hatching their eggs is to sneak them into other
birds' nests, and let those mama birds do all the work.

That's seriously rude. A few other bird and insect species engage in similar shame-
less behavior, but to find the most outrageous obligate brood parasite, you have to go
jump in a lake.

A female *cichlid* mouthbrooding newly hatched fish, which can be seen looking out her mouth

Specifically, Lake Tanganyika in Africa, where cuckoo catfish live. These conniving catfish share the lake with fish known as *cichlids* (SICK-lids). When the cichlids lay their eggs, cuckoo catfish rush in to gobble them up. At the same time, they lay eggs of their own. When the panicked cichlids sweep up their precious eggs to protect them, they grab some catfish eggs, too.

That's when things get truly cuckoo. Cichlids are "mouthbrooders," meaning they incubate and hatch their eggs in their mouths. So they swim around with a mouthful of catfish eggs along with their own, which is bad enough. But the cuckoo catfish eggs hatch before the cichlids, and their first meals are often the cichlid eggs the parents managed to save earlier. We know fish are cold-blooded. Apparently, cuckoo catfish are cold-hearted, too.

Squeaky Heels

The cuckoo catfish—scientific name *Synodontis multipunctatus* (sin-oh-DON-tuss mull-tee-PUNK-tot-us)—are also called "squeaker catfish," because they can make high-pitched squealing noises. Seems like it's the cichlids who should be squealing, but apparently not.

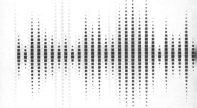

Strange
Burrowfellows

I f we're honest, burrowing owls aren't very well-named. They're owls, sure. That part is fine. But with a name like "burrowing owls," you'd expect the little birds to, you know, *burrow*.

But they don't. We guess they don't like to get their beaks dirty. Instead, most burrowing owls rely on other animals to do their digging for them. In the western part of the United States, it's usually prairie dogs. The prairie dogs—which do live on prairies, but aren't actually dogs, speaking of misleading names—dig huge interconnecting series of tunnels out in the grasslands. They do all that digging for their own benefit, of course. But the (not-so-) burrowing owl doesn't care. It's happy to swoop into a tunnel on the outskirts of a prairie dog colony and set up camp, like it owns the place. Maybe they should call it the "borrowing owl" instead.

It's a pretty good deal for the visitors. The owls get a place to live, protection from predators, a spot to nest, and even warnings from the prairie dogs when danger is nearby. Not bad for guests who showed up unannounced and didn't even bring a covered dish for dinner.

The situation isn't quite as rosy for the prairie dogs. They've got a tunnel they can't use anymore, and an owl interloper who "decorates" it with dried-up cow patties and other animal dung to attract flies and other insects that the owl eats. And you thought it was bad when your Aunt Betsy came to stay in the guest room. Just be happy you're not related to a burrowing owl.

Rattle Me This

Burrowing owls do have one potentially helpful trick to offer: When threatened in their borrowed burrows, they make a sound like a rattlesnake rattling its tail. This warning drives most predators away—from the owl, and hopefully from the nearby prairie dog colony, too.

Musca albina

Crooked Critters Quiz Answer

Musca albina is a species of fly known for this yucky habit:

a. Drinking sweat from horses for nutrients

b. Building nests out of shed human skin cells

c. **Laying eggs in poop balls rolled by beetles (correct)**

You'd think there are some things that should just be "hands off" even for crooks, but apparently not. Scarab beetles (a.k.a. dung beetles) eat a lot of poop, and they even roll animal feces into balls to save for later. The *Musca albina* flies take advantage of these cozy-looking dung balls by laying their eggs in them. When the young flies hatch, they have plenty of poop to eat. (Though everyone at the baby shower is sure going to wish they hatched in a bag of potpourri instead.)

Think About It

Some critters take from others to survive while other animals are more into recycling. For example, hermit crabs use old snail shells as homes. Can you think of any other organisms that "recycle" things that plants or animals (including humans) dispose of? If these critters made a pro-recycling poster for their species, what would it look like? Draw one up, just for fun!

Marabou stork

4 Disturbing the Peace

The wild is anything but quiet, but some critters make nightmare neighbors. Whether they're loud, rude, or just stinking up the joint, these brazen organisms will have any critter looking to move into a new zip code quick.

Take the Crooked Critters Quiz!

These baby birds are known for vomiting a foul-smelling glue at predators:
   a. Fulmars   b. Marabou storks   c. Peregrine falcons

Find out the answer at the end of the chapter!

Megaphone
Monkeys

Imagine you're in a library. You're trying to focus on your book, but people nearby are carrying on a loud conversation. You don't want to listen, but they're too loud to ignore. It's distracting, and you just want to tell those people to "shush."

In a large room, a loud person's voice might carry a few dozen feet. But there are "loud talkers" in the jungles of Central and South America, too. They're called *howler monkeys*, and their booming voices can carry for up to 3 miles. Just imagine all the "shushing" they get.

The howler monkeys howl at each other to keep track of their territory. This is important because they feed on jungle fruit and leaves. Too many monkeys in a small area could create a food shortage. So males in each troop of four to eight monkeys call out and listen for responses from other troops to determine how far away they are. These calls can be as loud as 140 decibels—louder than a rock concert or any human voice. It's about as loud as a jet engine 100 feet away.

Howlers can howl so loud because of a special bone in their throats called the *hyoid* (HI-oyd). Many animals, including humans, have a hyoid bone. But in howler monkeys, this bone is larger (compared to body size), and has a hollow space filled with air. This air chamber lets the sounds they make resonate, or echo, making the sounds coming out of their mouths louder. Much, much louder. Just hope you're not trying to read next to them when that happens.

Hazards for Howlers

Some species of howler monkey are threatened—but not because of loud conversations. Instead, the monkeys are sometimes killed by humans or caught as pets, and the jungles they live in are destroyed. Multiple species are listed as "endangered" or "vulnerable" by conservation groups.

49

The Bird That Thinks (and Stinks) Like a Cow

Hoatzins (HWAT-sins) are oddball birds by any standard. Members of the species live in and around the Amazon rainforest in South America, and as birds go, they don't seem to try very hard to fit in. They look sort of like chickens, but with longer turkey wings and tail, and a cockatoo mohawk hairdo. They also don't fly well. But their biggest difference is on the inside.

That's because hoatzins, unlike any other known bird species, exist on a diet of nothing but leaves. Those leaves contain tough plant matter called *cellulose* (SELL-you-lows), which the birds can't break down. Instead, they have compartments inside their stomachs that contain bacteria that can digest cellulose and that provide nutrients for the hoatzins that host them. This is exactly the same way that grass- and leaf-eating animals called *ruminants*—like cows, sheep, and deer—break down food. But hoatzins are the only known birds to do so.

That's where the stink comes in. Those active bacterial cultures sitting in the hoatzins guts produce gases—foul, smelly gases—as they break down food. The hoatzins belch those up, and generally make their entire surroundings smell terrible. Many people say the birds smell like manure. And that's never a compliment. Maybe someone could tell them about breath mints.

Hoatzin on Earth Are You Doing?

Hoatzins are so bad at flying, their young can't fly at all for 2 months after hatching. To compensate, mother hoatzins build nests on branches overhanging water. If the chicks are threatened, they drop out of the nest into the water, swim to shore and drag themselves back up the tree using claws along their wings. Basically, everything about hoatzins is strange.

51

The Rude Cuke
Who Spews Fruit

P lants of the cucumber species *Ecballium elaterium* (eck-BALL-ee-yum ee-LAH-tare-ee-yum) look perfectly peaceful, most of the time. But their mild-mannered stalks and unassuming fruit hide a messy secret that's hinted at in the plant's popular name: the squirting cucumber.

The fruits of these plants don't look like the cucumbers you'd buy in the grocery store—those are from a different species. Instead, they're smaller, around the size of your thumb, and covered in soft fuzzy "hairs" called *trichomes* (TRY-combs). As the fruits ripen, the seeds inside are bathed in a gooey green substance called *elaterium* (just like in the species name). The riper the fruit, the more green goo it holds—and the higher the pressure gets inside. That pressure can reach 3/4 of the atmospheric pressure we feel on the surface of the Earth, until . . . BLAMMO!

At the slightest disturbance—a brush from a fingertip, or a stiff wind—the fruit breaks off and shoots away, green sticky juice leaking out the back like a tiny rocket. The pods can travel at nearly 60 miles an hour, spitting goo and 20–40 seeds from the rear as it flies away.

This is great for the cucumber, because it spreads its seeds up to dozens of feet away. But it's no picnic for the unsuspecting animal or person nearby, covered in seed schmutz and scared out of their wits. Just be thankful those foot-long salad cukes aren't quite so explosive.

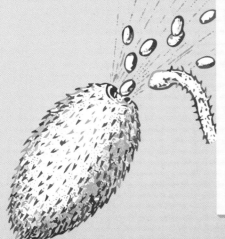

Step Away From the Cucumber

While squirting cucumber elaterium was used historically to treat various conditions, both the leaves and the fruit of the plant contain poisonous substances called *cucurbitacins* (CUE-cur-bit-ah-sins), and can cause stomach issues, swelling, and even death. So it's not safe to eat any part of the plant or to get the juice near the face or other sensitive areas.

Five Nights at Shrimpy's

S tealthy sharks cruise the waters in packs for their next meal. Ominous octopi and sneaky squids spread their tentacles to snatch an unsuspecting fish. But for one tiny sea creature, the thrill of the hunt is all about the jumpscare.

Snapping shrimp (also called *pistol shrimp*) live in coral and oyster reefs under the sea. They are less than 2 inches in length, but they make a noise that would burst your eardrums if you heard it. They have an asymmetrically long claw that snaps shut at more than 60 miles an hour and emits a sound of 220 decibels. A loud rock concert is about 110 decibels, and anything higher than 120 decibels can cause hearing loss in humans. The noise stuns their prey and also allows the shrimp to talk with each other (very, very, very loud talking).

It's quite fortunate for us that these shrimp live deep in the ocean where we can't

hear them snapping along to the chorus of "Under the Sea." (OK, they probably don't do that. Mostly because these shrimp are *definitely* on Team Ursula.) Yet, even with thousands of feet of water between us, these tiny crustaceans still manage to disturb our peace—a lot. Their loud snaps interrupt sonar technology, and their noise even prevented military personnel from detecting enemy submarines during World War II.

Snap to It

The shrimp's loud "snap" is actually caused by the motion of water, not just the two halves of the claws clinking together. When the claw snaps shut, a spike on one side slams into a hole on the other half, creating a shot of water. The speed of water creates bubbles, which pop and cause the sound. The snap is so powerful, it even causes a spark of light from the claw.

No Bark, All Bite

O n a list titled Critters That Should Only Exist in Nightmares, barking spiders are easily in the top five. The bad news? Yes, there is a spider called the barking spider. The good news? The name is wrong, because they don't actually bark. The not-really-good-but-somewhat-better-than-a-spider-that-barks news? These spiders still sound pretty darn creepy.

The barking spider is also named the Queensland whistling spider. Like several other Australian tarantula species, it makes a sound when provoked by rubbing special hairs—called *setae*—against its mouthpiece. The noise doesn't really sound like whistling either—more like a humming or buzzing. The people who name these things really need to clean the wax out of their ears.

Barking spider

Despite being "loud and proud" arachnids, whistling spiders are quite shy. They rarely leave their burrows, which is understandable, since it's basically a tarantula mansion. They build humongous silk burrows up to 2 meters deep—about the height of your bedroom's door—and they hide in an area with an air pocket that can keep them oxygenated for several

Fangs of a huntsman spider

days. If you're foolish enough to disturb them, they have one heck of a bite. So if you are alone in Australia and you hear a sinister hum, you might want to check to see if a not-so-itsy-bitsy-spider is crawling up your waterspout.

Giant huntsman spider

Supersized Spiders

Humans commonly call any large spider a tarantula, but this is not quite accurate. The spider with the largest leg span in the world is a non-tarantula spider. It's called the *giant huntsman spider*, and it has a leg span of one foot—about the size of a dinner plate!

Fulmar

58

Crooked Critters Quiz Answer

These baby birds are known for vomiting a foul-smelling glue at predators:

a. **Fulmars (correct)**
b. Marabou storks
c. Peregrine falcons

Baby fulmar birds are completely exposed to many birds of prey, so they need a way to defend themselves. And boy, do they have a doozy. They spew a sticky, fish-smelling vomit about 5 feet. The vomit doesn't wash off, so predatory birds that get it on their wings may never be able to fly again.

Think About It

This chapter was about organisms that make a ruckus, but not all critters are known for causing a commotion. Can you think of any animals known for being stealthy and silent?

Venus fly trap with caught fly

5 Maniacs and Madmen

All critters do what they need to do to survive, but some of the things they do sure seem to be plucked out of the pages of a horror novel. These nightmare critters cause other animals to quake in their boots, and you might let out a few shrieks yourself if you dare to flip through these pages. Consider yourself warned.

Take the Crooked Critters Quiz!

These carnivorous plants team up with assassin bugs to capture and digest prey.

a. Roridula plants   b. Venus fly traps   c. Portuguese sundew plants

Find out the answer at the end of the chapter!

The 46-Legged Noose

The humid Amazon rainforest is home to the ultimate creepy crawly—a giant centipede by the name of *Scolopendra gigantea*. It's the world's largest living centipede species, stretching up to one foot in length, and its up to 23 pairs of fire-yellow legs do more than give everyone a bad case of the heebie jeebies. (Although . . . mission accomplished. Color us heebied and jeebied.) Their multilegged bodies allow them to speed through the jungle so they can sneak up and snatch unsuspecting prey.

This giant centipede feeds on anything it can take down—tarantulas, snakes, and rats are all part of its menu. But when it's in the mood for some *really* fast food, it hangs upside down from the ceilings of caves and snatches bats flying by. Its hind legs are powerful enough to anchor it to the ceiling while the rest of its body dangles down. The bat can't see it, so it flies right into a 46-legged trap. As soon as the bat makes contact, the centipede wraps its legs around it and injects it with an extremely potent venom that kills it almost instantly. If a person ended up on the wrong side of this centipede's fangs, the venom is not likely to cause any long-term harm, but people who have suffered a bite have described the pain to be as bad as a broken bone.

Any critter that makes both Dracula and Batman watch their necks is definitely a bad seed. Yikes.

Fifty Pairs of Tennis Shoes?

The word *centipede* means "100-footed," but this is a misnomer. Depending on the species, centipedes can have as few as 15 pairs of legs or more than 170 pairs.

Brown centipede

A Very
Bad Day for
Spidey

Tarantulas strike fear in the hearts of many, and their hairy bodies and big fangs are enough to make your skin crawl. Ironically, these creepy critters have a lot more to fear from their fellow crawlies than we do—specifically, the tarantula hawk wasp.

If just about any other insect crossed the path of a tarantula, it would become a very fast meal. The tarantula hawk wasp, however, is more than ready for the fight. When female wasps are ready to lay eggs, they go out in search of these giant spiders, strumming their webs to draw them out. The spider dashes out, ready to bite the intruder with its venom-filled fangs. A duel commences, but the tarantula hawk wasp has a secret weapon. When the spider rears up on its hind legs, the wasp pierces the tarantula's soft abdomen with its stinger. The sting doesn't kill the tarantula, but it has a potent venom that paralyzes it. The wasp then drags the tarantula across the ground—often over great distances—to its burrow where it lays its eggs inside of the spider's abdomen. When the eggs hatch, the wasp young eat the paralyzed tarantula alive.

So, remember—you don't have to *like* that spider lurking in the corner of your bedroom ceiling, but at least it's probably not thinking about implanting tiny spiders into you. And for that you can be grateful.

My, That Stings!

The tarantula hawk is a bit scary to humans, too, because it has a terrible sting. An entomologist named Justin O. Schmidt created his famous Schmidt Pain Scale to rate the pain he experienced after being stung by many different insects. He ranked the tarantula hawk wasp as the second worst sting on the planet, after the bullet ant.

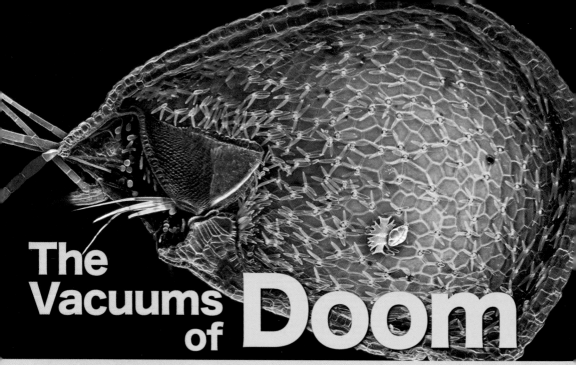

The Vacuums of Doom

We're not sure what the most terrifying death in nature would be. But here's a scenario that's likely high on that list: Imagine you're swimming, minding your own aquatic business. In the blink of an eye—actually, 10 times faster, as quick as 1/30th of a second—you're sucked into a see-through chamber in a huge wave of water. You can see freedom through the chamber walls, but the opening has already resealed shut. Slowly, the water pumps back out, and digestive enzymes seep in. Occasionally, more water—and victims—rush in, but there's no way to escape. Over hours or days, the enzymes will break everything in the chamber down into basic nutrients.

It may sound like a scene from Edgar Allan Poe's nightmares, but it plays out in ponds and bogs across the world, thanks to plants known as *bladderworts*. These macabre murderers belong to more than 200 species of *Utricularia* (you-trick-you-LAR-ee-uh), the largest group of carnivorous plants. Venus flytraps get more press, but bladderworts are the real silent assassins.

Water-dwelling bladderworts grow bladders, each of which is a trap in waiting. By pumping water out of the bladder, the plant creates a vacuum inside. When hair-like structures outside the bladder are disturbed by a passing critter, the bladder opens and water rushes in to fill the vacuum, sweeping the animal inside, too. The animals can survive inside—for a while—but the digestive enzymes pumped in eventually take care of that. We think Poe would be proud.

The World of Worts

Bladderworts can live in muddy soil as well as fresh water, and have spread to every continent except Antarctica. If you pull a bladderwort out of the water, you may hear a series of crackling noises as the traps snap shut.

A Hair(worm)y Situation

Grasshoppers are great jumpers, but terrible swimmers. Because they can't swim—and nobody makes tiny insect-sized water wings to help them out—grasshoppers tend to avoid large bodies of water. Except the ones that seek out water in the middle of the night and jump right in, with no way to get out. Why would they do that? Are there midnight grasshopper pool parties?

Not quite. Those grasshoppers have been infected by a species of parasitic hairworm called *Spinochordodes tellinii* (spin-oe-core-DOE-days tell-een-EE-eye). A grasshopper (or cricket) can accidentally eat the larvae of the worm, which start out small, but don't stay that way. Once inside a grasshopper, a larva can grow into an adult worm, three to four times the length of the insect it calls home. That causes obvious issues for the poor grasshopper, but the hairworm has a problem, too.

To lay eggs and complete its life cycle, the worm must get back into water—where grasshoppers literally fear to tread. So adult hairworms alter the central nervous systems of the grasshoppers hosting them and override their natural fear of water. These grasshoppers may even seek out water—usually during nighttime—and hop right in. When they do, the worms they host escape and swim away, but the brainwashed grasshoppers can't get out and drown. Maybe somebody should look into making those little water wings, after all.

Your Proteins, or Mine?

Scientists have found that adult hairworms produce proteins similar to those found in grasshoppers and crickets. The worms also can affect which proteins are produced in their hosts' central nervous systems, which may help to explain how the worms affect their hosts' behavior.

Some Fungi Are No Fun at All

There's nothing wrong with a good fungus. Mushrooms, yeast, penicillin mold, truffles—these are all nice sorts of fungi. And then there are the 400 or so fungus species in the group called *Cordyceps* (CORE-de-seps), which

Cordyceps species are parasites that invade insects, spiders, and sometimes, other fungi. Spores of the fungus attach to a host and begin to grow. Long, spiky growths shoot from the spores, forming finger-like extensions that can be longer than the infected animal itself.

That's not especially nice. But it's also not the worst part.

The bigger problem for a *Cordyceps*-afflicted animal is that the fungus doesn't just grow out—it also grows in. Those spikes pierce inside the insect or spider, slowly replacing tissues and organs with fungus. Eventually, this kills the animal, leaving the fungus growing from the empty husk of hard exoskeleton the bug used to call home. Soon, the fungus will release new spores, starting the cycle anew. Like we said: not so nice.

Some species of *Cordyceps* even practice a bit of mind control. Some ant-invading fungi release chemicals that control the behavior of their hosts. The invaders release chemicals in certain ants' brains, which lead those "zombie ants" to move to a location ideal for the fungus to release a new set of spores.

A Friend in Fungus?

Though *Cordyceps* are pretty nasty for their hosts, humans have put the fungi to good use. Traditional Asian healers have used *Cordyceps* in treatments for hundreds of years, and modern studies suggest products from the fungus may indeed have medicinal properties.

The sticky leaves of the Roridula
plant with caught fly

Think About It

Many organisms seem scary or yucky to humans, but they are actually really cool when you learn more about them. Pick an organism that you think gets a bad rap and try to find 10 interesting facts about it. If you like what you find, put the facts together with pictures of the critter in a collage that you can hang in your room!

Crooked Critters Quiz Answer

These carnivorous plants team up with assassin bugs to capture and digest prey:

a. **Roridula plants (correct)**
b. Venus fly traps
c. Portuguese Sundew plants

Roridula plants have a big digestive problem. In fact, it's so big that they are not really classified as true carnivorous plants. They can trap insects in their sticky hairs, but they lack the ability to digest the bug. The assassin bug, however, can navigate the plant's hairs without getting stuck. It eats the trapped insect and then excretes feces all over the plant. The plant absorbs nutrients from the buggy meal from the assassin bug's poop. What a pal, huh?

Whistling duck

6 Identity Thieves and Frauds

Walking around as a clone of someone else sounds like something straight out of a science fiction movie, but it's just a normal day in the wild. All of the critters in this chapter pull the wool over the eyes of other critters by pretending to be someone else.

Take the Crooked Critters Quiz!

These birds mimic the alarm cries of meerkats to steal their food:

a. Drongos   b. Cape crows   c. Whistling ducks

Find out the answer at the end of the chapter!

The Perks of Being a Corpse Flower

Humans are always making a stink about how we . . . well . . . stink. We roll on the deodorant, spritz on the perfume, and always keep a breath mint handy in case the cafeteria puts a bit too much garlic in the Chef's Surprise. Other organisms don't even try to hide their bad-to-the-bone B.O. One of the most notorious (and noxious) examples is the oh-so-truthfully named corpse flower.

At first glance, the corpse flower looks deceptively inviting. Its scientific name is *Titan arum*, and it certainly doesn't disappoint on the titan part. The plant's massive flower structure grows taller than a human (the largest one is more than 10 feet tall), and while it looks like one gigantic flower, its stalk contains many tiny buds. But do they ever stink. Taking a whiff will fill your nostrils with a putrid aroma of rotten meat, raw fish, dirty socks, and garbage.

These flowers are not likely to appear in a lot of Mother's Day bouquets, but their horrific stench does attract flies and dung beetles, which the flower relies on for pollination. The flower goes all in on the gag, too. Its rust-red color fools these rot-loving bugs into thinking it's a dead animal, and the flower can even raise its temperature to superpower its stench. With those kinds of special effects, could a TV show named *The Flowering Dead* be far behind?

Grossest Perfume on the Planet

The Chicago Botanic Garden wanted to know what exactly makes the corpse flower stink so badly, so they analyzed the chemicals produced by their own plant (a corpse flower named "Spike"). They found that the plant produced the same chemicals that cause the stinky smells of onions, Limburger cheese, rotted fish, and sweaty feet.

I'm Not a Queen, But I Play One on Ant-TV

Ants are tiny, but in a group they can kill much bigger organisms. Entering an ant colony is certain death for most wayward critters, but the caterpillar that becomes the Large Blue butterfly waltzes in like it owns the place. And for an entire year, it pretty much does.

This particular caterpillar survives by fooling ants into thinking it is their queen. After hatching, it secretes chemicals that smell like a very specific species of red ant. When an ant comes along, it assumes the caterpillar is a lost ant larva, so it carries the caterpillar inside the colony. Once inside, the caterpillar mimics the sounds of the queen ants, ensuring that it receives the finest in ant pampering. The worker ants bend over backward to tend to the phony queen, often at great expense to the colony. Some of these caterpillars will eat the ants' own larvae for food.

The caterpillar mooches off the ants for about a year, before forming a cocoon. Even inside the cocoon, the developing butterfly continues to make ant sounds, so the ants will leave it alone. When the butterfly emerges, the cat's out of the bag, and the ants will usually try to attack it. But it's too late. The butterfly has scales that protect it from ant bites, so it crawls out of the colony—sometimes being carried by the ants—and makes a quick getaway without ever being charged with its year-long identity fraud.

Formica rufa workers

Big Ol' Babies

Large Blue caterpillars are some of the most high-maintenance babies in the animal kingdom. It's estimated that more than 200 ant larvae and more than 350 worker ants are required to keep a single caterpillar alive!

Pay
No Attention
to the
Spider Behind
the Spider

Most of the organisms in this chapter steal the identity of other species, but there is one critter that takes things a step too far—it steals its own identity. A newly discovered spider in the Amazon builds a fake spider in its web that is five times larger than itself.

Interestingly, it was the decoy spider that caught the scientists' attention in the first place. They initially thought the decoy was a dead spider in the web, until they looked closer to see a much tinier spider assembling this giant spider clone. It uses leaves, sticks, and dead parts of prey to build the elaborate decoy, which has a head, body, and legs, just like a real spider.

Scientists aren't exactly sure why these spiders build a decoy at all, but it most likely helps them to avoid predators, possibly damselflies, which feast on small spiders but tend to avoid large ones. The spider is thought to belong to a genus called *Cyclosa*, a group of spiders known for using debris and insect parts in their web, usually for camouflage. Scientists recently discovered that a few *Cyclosa* species on other continents also build decoys in their webs, but nothing quite as elaborate as this little Amazonian spider. For now, this convincing fraud remains a mystery.

Not Exactly Fashionistas

We do know one thing about these Amazonian spiders—they are not a fan of sparkles. A group of researchers wondered if the spider would build decoys with any material that was available, so they dumped glitter into their webs. The spiders snipped all of the glitter out, and most likely scoffed at the scientists for their tacky taste in webbing.

Photinus pyralis

Why Lie, Firefly?

Depending on where you live, you may be treated on summer evenings to one of nature's greatest light shows—fireflies (or if you prefer, lightning bugs) flashing signals at each other in the summer twilight. Male fireflies start the signals, showing off for the females. If a female firefly likes what she sees, she'll signal back, and the pair may eventually meet and mate.

At least, that's how it's supposed to work. But some sneaky insects break the rules.

Consider two types of firefly, called *Photinus* (FOE-tin-us) and *Photuris* (FOE-tour-is). *Photuris* females watch for their males' mating signals, but they keep an antenna

The Firefly Double-Switcheroo

Not to be outdone, male *Photuris* fireflies also have a trick up their, uh, phosphorescent butts. The males have learned how to send mating signals that *Photinus* males would make, but not because they're hungry. They're actually trying to trick a *Photuris* female into thinking she's lured in a *Photinus* victim, when it's really a *Photuris* male who's hoping to mate with her.

out for those from *Photinus* males, too. What's more, the crafty *Photuris* females know how to flash back a response the lonely *Photinus* male expects from a female of its own species—so the male comes flying over to say hello. (After he checks his hair in the mirror and pops a tiny breath mint.)

Sadly for him, the *Photuris* female isn't who he thinks she is. And she's not interested in romance; she's just looking for a free dinner. Namely, him. *Photuris* females prey on *Photinus* fireflies, and their main strategy is luring the would-be loverflies over with just the right sets of flashing lights. Why go out to eat, when the meal will come running to you?

This Mummy's No Dummy

"**M**ummy berry" sounds like something you might get while trick-or-treating on Halloween. But hopefully, it isn't. Because mummy berry is actually a disease caused by a species of fungus called *Monilinia vaccinii-corymbosi* (moan-ah-LYN-ee-ah vack-SIN-ee-eye core-em-BOE-see).

Like many forest fungi, this one begins life as spores. The spores are released from cup-like structures on the ground, hoping to land on a nice blueberry plant. When one does, it grows a nasty fuzz on the blueberry's leaves—as fungi do. But then it gets shifty.

To spread itself as far as possible, the fungus makes the affected leaves seep sugars, which smell sweet and emit ultraviolet light. Both of these make the sickly leaves resemble a flower to pollinating insects like bees. They land on the leaves looking for nectar—in the process, picking up spores, which they carry to other plants and flowers.

When a spore is carried to a blueberry flower, it's very careful about settling into its new home. If the fungus spread too aggressively, the plant would fight back. Instead, the fungus behaves just like a grain of blueberry pollen. This gets it free passage into the plant's developing fruit, full of nutrients, and that's where the name comes in. "Mummy berries" on an infected blueberry plant are shriveled and gray as though they're dead, but they're white inside, from the fungus growing through them, right from the center. That's a neat trick—but hardly a treat.

Curse of the Mummy Berry

Mummy berry disease can be a real problem for commercial blueberry growers. Outbreaks across North America have led to up to 80% crop loss in individual fields, and cost farmers hundreds of thousands of dollars. Luckily, some blueberry varieties are resistant.

85

Drongo

Crooked Critters Quiz Answer

These birds mimic the alarm cries of meerkats to steal their food:

a. **Drongos (correct)**
b. Cape crows
c. Whistling ducks

Drongos don't exactly look like criminals, but they are as sneaky as they come. They can mimic the warning calls of other birds and meerkats, causing them to drop their meal and scamper. The drongo then scoops up the abandoned meal.

Think About It

On stage and on film, actors often play animal characters. If you wrote a play in which all of the characters were animals, which animals would you choose? What would it be about? What traits does each animal have that the actors will have to mimic?

Burrowing owl

Bibliography

Introduction

Biology Reference. (n.d.). *Adaptation*. Retrieved from http://www.biology reference.com/A-Ar/Adaptation.html

McGinley, M. (2014). Interspecific competition. *The Encyclopedia of Earth*. Retrieved from http://www.eoearth.org/view/article/153873/

Understanding Evolution. (n.d.). *Adaptation*. Retrieved from http://evolution.berkeley.edu/evolibrary/article/evo_31

Chapter 1

Big Bad Bullies

Canales, R., & Mancosky, A. (2014). *Dicrocoelium dendriticum: Interactions.* Retrieved from https://bioweb.uwlax.edu/bio203/s2014/canales_ross/interactions.htm

Centers for Disease Control and Prevention. (2013). *Bed bugs FAQs.* Retrieved from http://www.cdc.gov/parasites/bedbugs/faqs.html

Centers for Disease Control and Prevention. (2013). *Dicrocoeliasis.* Retrieved from http://www.cdc.gov/dpdx/dicrocoeliasis/index.html

Davidson, S. (2004). Dwarf mistletoe: Parasitic plant wreaks havoc. *LiveScience.* Retrieved from http://www.livescience.com/3757-dwarf-mistletoe-parasitic-plant-wreaks-havoc.html

Encyclopedia Britannica. (2014). *Mistletoe.* Retrieved from http://www.britannica.com/plant/mistletoe

Hayden, T. (2010). Infecting a snail: Life cycle of the grossest parasite. *WIRED.* Retrieved from http://www.wired.com/2010/05/process_snail

Hogenboom, M. (2015). Origin of bed bugs revealed. *BBC.* Retrieved from http://www.bbc.com/earth/story/20150130-origin-of-bed-bugs-revealed

Jemison, M. (2014). Crazy eyes and mind control—The power of parasites. *Smithsonian Insider.* Retrieved from http://smithsonianscience.si.edu/2014/11/crazy-eyes-mind-control-power-parasites

Lafontaine, S., Gallagher, K., Bombard, J., Anima, D., & Zhang, D. (2016). Microbiology: Zombie ants with Dicrocoelium dendriticum. *The Towers.* Retrieved from http://towers.wpi.edu/read/4279/microbiology-zombie-ants-with-dicrocoelium-dendriticum

Macnab, V., & Barber, I. (2011). Some (worms) like it hot: Fish parasites grow faster in warmer water, and alter host thermal preferences. *Global Change Biology, 18,* 1540–1548.

Petruzzello, M. (2016). Editor picks: Top 5 most awesome parasitic plants. *Encyclopedia Britannica*. Retrieved from https://www.britannica.com/list/top-5-most-awesome-parasitic-plants

The Phrase Finder. (n.d.). *Sleep tight*. Retrieved from http://www.phrases.org.uk/meanings/sleep-tight.html

Sutherland, A. M., Choe, D.-H., & Lewis, V. R. (2013). *Bed bugs*. Retrieved from http://www.ipm.ucdavis.edu/PMG/PESTNOTES/pn7454.html

Tainter, F. H. (2002). What does mistletoe have to do with Christmas? *APSNet Features*. Retrieved from http://www.apsnet.org/publications/apsnetfeatures/pages/mistletoe.aspx

Wesołowska, W., & Wesołowski, T. (2013). Do Leucochloridium sporocysts manipulate the behaviour of their snail hosts? *Journal of Zoology, 292,* 151–155.

Yong, E. (2011). Some like it hot (if they're riddled with parasites). *National Geographic*. Retrieved from http://phenomena.nationalgeographic.com/2011/11/17/tapeworm-stickleback-parasite-heat

Yong, E. (2013). New study upholds reputation of classic parasite. *National Geographic*. Retrieved from http://phenomena.nationalgeographic.com/2013/12/02/new-study-upholds-reputation-of-classic-parasite

Chapter 2

Mobsters

Bittel, J. (2016). The Christmas crab massacre. *Pacific Standard*. Retrieved from http://www.psmag.com/nature-and-technology/the-christmas-crab-massacre

Davies, E. (2011). Reef fish live and hunt as a team. *BBC*. Retrieved from http://www.bbc.co.uk/nature/15261196

Goldman, J. G. (2016). Meet the spiders that have formed armies 50,000 strong. *BBC*. Retrieved from http://www.bbc.com/earth/story/20160122-meet-the-spiders-that-have-formed-armies-50000-strong

Guilford, G. (2013). Jellyfish are taking over the seas, and it might be too late to stop them. *Quartz*. Retrieved from http://qz.com/133251/jellyfish-are-taking-over-the-seas-and-it-might-be-too-late-to-stop-them

Holmes, B. (2015). Orcas seen in unique group ambush-and-kill attack on dolphins. *New Scientist*. Retrieved from https://www.newscientist.com/article/dn28621-orcas-seen-in-unique-group-ambush-and-kill-attack-on-dolphins

Howell, E. (2013). Will jellyfish rule the ocean? *Discovery News*. Retrieved from http://news.discovery.com/earth/oceans/will-jellyfish-rule-the-ocean-131106.htm

Humphrys, L. (2015). *Wasp import set to save Christmas Island*. Retrieved from http://www.latrobe.edu.au/news/articles/2015/release/wasp-import-set-to-save-christmas-island

Kaplan, M. (2007). Unique orca hunting technique documented. *Nature*. Retrieved from http://www.nature.com/news/2007/071214/full/news.2007.380.html

Kiyohara, S., Sakata, Y., Yoshitomi, T., & Tsukahara, J. (2002). The 'goatee' of goatfish: innervation of taste buds in the barbels and their representation in the brain. *Proceedings of the Royal Society B: Biological Sciences, 269,* 1773–1780.

Minogue, K. (2013). Deadly tricks of spiders without webs. *Shorelines*. Retrieved from http://sercblog.si.edu/?p=4371

Morell, V. (2015). How orcas work together to whip up a meal. *National Geographic*. Retrieved from http://ngm.nationalgeographic.com/2015/07/orca-feeding/morell-text

National Geographic. (2012). *Red crab migration*. Retrieved from http://education.nationalgeographic.org/media/red-crab-migration

Nature on PBS. (2014). *The killer whale's killer weapon—Its brain*. Retrieved from http://www.pbs.org/wnet/nature/killer-whales-killer-weapon-brain/11352

Nature on PBS. (2015). Social spiders spin massive nest. Retrieved from https://www.youtube.com/watch?v=td09PIjz0iQ

Orchard, M. (2013). *Red crab breeding migration*. Retrieved, from http://www.christmasislandcrabs.com/#!red-crab-migration/c23me

O'Rourke, M. (2016). The power of the jellyfish. *Risk Management*. Retrieved from http://www.rmmagazine.com/2013/11/01/the-power-of-the-jellyfish

Parks Australia. (n.d.). *Red crabs*. Retrieved from http://www.parksaustralia.gov.au/christmas/people-place/red-crabs.html

Spiegel Online. (2007). *Jellied salmon: Scientists mystified by jellyfish attacks on fish farm*. Retrieved from http://www.spiegel.de/international/europe/jellied-salmon-scientists-mystified-by-jellyfish-attacks-on-fish-farm-a-519666.html

Vince, G. (2012). Jellyfish blooms creating oceans of slime. *BBC*. Retrieved from http://www.bbc.com/future/story/20120405-blooming-jellyfish-problems

The Wilderness Society. (2015). *Yellow crazy ants on Christmas Island*. Retrieved from https://www.wilderness.org.au/articles/yellow-crazy-ants-christmas-island

Yong, E. (2011). Reef alliances: goatfish hunt in packs, while groupers team up with moray eels. *Discover*. Retrieved from http://blogs.discovermagazine.com/notrocketscience/2011/10/24/reef-alliances-goatfish-hunt-in-packs-while-groupers-team-up-with-moray-eels/#.Vtw78jjltjo

Zielinski, S. (2011). The fish that hunt like lions. *Smithsonian Magazine*. Retrieved from http://www.smithsonianmag.com/ist/?next=/science-nature/the-fish-that-hunt-like-lions-479311

Chapter 3

Breaking and Entering

Australian Government Department of the Environment. (n.d.). *South polar skua*. Retrieved from http://www.antarctica.gov.au/about-antarctica/wildlife/animals/flying-birds/south-polar-skua

BBC. (2005). *Diner discovers exotic parasite*. Retrieved from http://news.bbc.co.uk/2/hi/uk_news/england/london/4205538.stm

Cohen, M. S. (2015). *Host-parasite interactions of the African cuckoo catfish (Synodontis multipunctatus)* (Doctoral dissertation). Retrieved from ProQuest Dissertation and Theses—Gradworks. (Publication No. 3721790)

Evolution of squeaker catfishes in Africa's Lake Tanganyika [Weblog post]. (2009). Retrieved from http://scienceblogs.com/grrlscientist/2009/03/25/evolution-of-african-synodonti

Ferguson, C. (2014). Squatting owls eavesdrop on prairie dogs. *Inside Science*. Retrieved from https://www.insidescience.org/content/squatting-owls-eavesdrop-prairie-dogs/1535

Johnsgard, P. (2006, Jan./Feb.). The howdy owl and the prairie dog. *Birding*, 40–44. Retrieved from https://www.aba.org/birding/v38n1p40.pdf

Kaufman, K. (n.d.). Burrowing owl. *Audubon*. Retrieved from https://www.audubon.org/field-guide/bird/burrowing-owl

Kaufman, K. (n.d.). South polar skua. *Audubon*. Retrieved from https://www.audubon.org/field-guide/bird/south-polar-skua

Laidre, M. E. (n.d.). The social lives of hermits. *Natural History Magazine*. Retrieved from http://www.naturalhistorymag.com/features/122719/the-social-lives-of-hermits

National Geographic. (n.d.). *Arctic skua*. Retrieved from http://animals.nationalgeographic.com/animals/birds/arctic-skua

National Wildlife Federation. (n.d.). *Burrowing owl.* Retrieved from https://www. nwf.org/Wildlife/Wildlife-Library/Birds/Burrowing-Owl.aspx

NOVA. (2009). *Are you my mother?* Retrieved from http://www.pbs.org/wgbh/ nova/sciencenow/0407/03-moth-nf.html

Oklahoma Department of Wildlife Conservation. (n.d.). *Burrowing owl.* Retrieved from http://www.wildlifedepartment.com/wildlifemgmt/species/ burrowingowl.htm

Paulus, S. (2015). Meet a hermit crab who has shacked up in a Lego. *Smithsonian Magazine.* Retrieved from http://www.smithsonianmag.com/smart-news/ meet-hermit-crab-who-has-shacked-lego-180954902

Provenzano, A., Jr. (Ed.). (2016). *The biology of crustacea: Pathobiology.* New York, NY: Academic Press.

Smithsonian Ocean Portal. (2012). *Marine parasites: Crazy . . . and really cool!* Retrieved from http://ocean.si.edu/blog/marine-parasites-crazy%E2%80%A 6and-really-cool

Stromberg, J. (2014). 14 fun facts about sea hawks. *Smithsonian Magazine.* Retrieved from http://www.smithsonianmag.com/science-nature/14-fun- facts-about-sea-hawks-180949528

Williams, J. (2016). *The not so lonely lives of hermit crabs: Studies on hermit crab symbionts.* Hofstra University. Retrieved from http://www.hofstra.edu/pdf/ ORSP_Williams_Fall03.pdf

Zimmer, C. (2013). Tongue-eating fish parasites never cease to amaze. *National Geographic.* Retrieved from http://phenomena.nationalgeographic.com/ 2013/02/28/tongue-eating-fish-parasites-never-cease-to-amaze

Zollinger, S. A. (2009). *The cuckoo catfish.* Retrieved from http://indianapublic media.org/amomentofscience/excuse-baby-mout

Chapter 4

Disturbing the Peace

BBC Earth Unplugged. (2013). *Exploding cucumbers!—Slo mo #36—Earth unplugged.* Retrieved from https://www.youtube.com/watch?v=wOIHzl2h9a8

The Belize Zoo. (n.d.). *Black howler monkey.* Retrieved from http://www.belize zoo.org/mammals/black-howler-monkey.html

Centers for Disease Control and Prevention. (2015). *About sound.* Retrieved from http://www.cdc.gov/ncbddd/hearingloss/sound.html

Deatrick, E. (2015). The hoatzin: Misfit, belcher, genetic mystery. *Audubon.* Retrieved from https://www.audubon.org/news/hoatzin

Dunn, T. (n.d.). *The loudest animal in the new world.* Retrieved from https://nationalzoo.si.edu/animals/smallmammals/exhibits/howlermonkeys/loudestanimal

Encyclopedia Britannica. (n.d.). *Tarantula.* Retrieved from http://www.britannica.com/animal/tarantula

Leutwyler, K. (2000). Snapping shrimp. *Scientific American.* Retrieved from http://www.scientificamerican.com/article/snapping-shrimp

Lewes, D. (1951). Observations on the internal pressure of the ripening fruit of *Ecballium Elaterium. Kew Bulletin, 6,* 443–444. Retrieved from http://www.jstor.org/stable/4118024?seq=1#page_scan_tab_contents

Naish, D. (2011). Hoatzins are no longer exclusively South American and once crossed an ocean. *Scientific American.* Retrieved from http://blogs.scientificamerican.com/tetrapod-zoology/hoatzins-in-africa

National Geographic. (n.d.). *Howler monkey.* Retrieved, from http://animals.nationalgeographic.com/animals/mammals/howler-monkey

Parry, J. (2011). Hoatzin: Meet the stink bird. *Discover Wildlife.* Retrieved from http://www.discoverwildlife.com/animals/hoatzin-meet-stink-bird

Queensland Museum. (n.d.). *Tarantula or whistling spiders.* Retrieved from http://www.qm.qld.gov.au/Find+out+about/Animals+of+Queensland/ Spiders/Primitive+Spiders+Infraorder+Mygalomorphae/Tarantula+or+ Whistling+Spiders#.VsSUJzjltjo

Reshanov, A. (2014). Lifeform of the week: Hoatzin. *EarthSky.* Retrieved from http://earthsky.org/earth/lifeform-of-the-week-hoatzins-are-odd-birds

Roach, J. (2001). Snapping shrimp stun prey with flashy bang. *National Geographic.* Retrieved from http://news.nationalgeographic.com/news/2001/10/1003_ SnappingShrimp.html

Sci-News.com. (2014). *Hoatzin: South American bird may have originated in Europe* Retrieved from http://www.sci-news.com/paleontology/science-hoatzin-bird-europe-01713.html

The Scotsman. (2010). *Exploding cucumbers . . . how cool are they?* Retrieved from http://www.scotsman.com/news/exploding-cucumbers-how-cool-are-they-1-1245696

Smithsonian Marine Station at Fort Pierce. (n.d.). *Snapping shrimp.* Retrieved from http://www.sms.si.edu/IRLFieldGuide/Alpheu_hetero.htm

Thompson, H. (2015). Inside the roaring sex lives of howler monkeys. *Science News.* Retrieved from https://www.sciencenews.org/article/inside-roaring-sex-lives-howler-monkeys

Thuilier, C. (2012). Australian spiders: The 10 most dangerous. *Australian Geographic.* Retrieved from http://www.australiangeographic.com.au/topics/ wildlife/2012/08/australian-spiders-the-10-most-dangerous

Versluis, M. (2000). How snapping shrimp snap: Through cavitating bubbles. *Science, 289,* 2114–2117.

Whyte, R., & Anderson, G. (n.d.). *Phlogius crassipes Queensland whistling tarantula.* Retrieved from http://www.arachne.org.au/01_cms/details.asp? ID=2411

Chapter 5

Maniacs and Madmen

Animal Planet. (n.d.). *Death crawler.* Retrieved from http://www.animalplanet. com/tv-shows/lost-tapes/creatures/death-crawler

BBC Nature. (2014). *Cordyceps.* Retrieved from http://www.bbc.co.uk/nature/ life/Cordyceps

Bhattacharya, S. (2005). Parasites brainwash grasshoppers into death dive. *New Scientist.* Retrieved from https://www.newscientist.com/article/dn7927-parasites-brainwash-grasshoppers-into-death-dive

Biron, D., Marche, L., Ponton, F., Loxdale, H., Galeotti, N., Renault, L. . . . Thomas, F. (2005). Behavioural manipulation in a grasshopper harbouring hairworm: A proteomics approach. *Proceedings of the Royal Society B: Biological Sciences, 272,* 2117–2126.

Botanical Society of America. (n.d.). *Utricularia—The bladderwort.* Retrieved from http://botany.org/Carnivorous_Plants/Utricularia.php

Castro, J. (2014). Zombie fungus enslaves only its favorite ant brains. *LiveScience.* Retrieved from http://www.livescience.com/47751-zombie-fungus-picky-about-ant-brains.html

Crawford, Z. (2010). *Parasite of the day: March 31—Spinochordodes tellinii.* Retrieved from http://dailyparasite.blogspot.com/2010/03/march-31-spino chordodes-tellinii.html

Davis, L. (2012). Fungal infection causes tarantula to grow antlers. *io9.* Retrieved from http://io9.gizmodo.com/5918948/fungal-infection-causes-tarantula-to-grow-antlers

Gordon, E. (n.d.). *A teacher's resource guide to millipedes & centipedes.* Retrieved from http://blogs.cornell.edu/naturalistoutreach/files/2013/09/Millipedes-CentipedesGuide-2jubwdz.pdf

Hill, K. (2013). The fungus that reduced humanity to the last of us. *Scientific American*. Retrieved from http://blogs.scientificamerican.com/but-not-simpler/the-fungus-that-reduced-humanity-to-the-last-of-us

International Carnivorous Plant Society. (n.d.). *The genus Utricularia*. Retrieved from http://www.carnivorousplants.org/cp/Genera/Utricularia.php

Kaplan, M. (2011). Photos: "Zombie" ants found with new mind-control fungi. *National Geographic*. Retrieved from http://news.nationalgeographic.com/news/2011/03/pictures/110303-zombie-ants-fungus-new-species-fungi-bugs-science-brazil

Meshew, C. (2001). *Scolopendra gigantea*. Retrieved from http://animaldiversity.org/accounts/Scolopendra_gigantea

National Park Service. (n.d.). *Tarantulas and tarantula hawks*. Retrieved from http://www.nps.gov/band/learn/nature/tarantulas-and-tarantula-hawks.htm

Panda, A., & Swain, K. (2011). Traditional uses and medicinal potential of Cordyceps sinensis of Sikkim. *Journal of Ayurveda and Integrative Medicine, 2*(1), 9.

Rice, B. (2009). *The carnivorous plant FAQ: Utricularia*. Retrieved from http://www.sarracenia.com/faq/faq5580.html

Simaiakis, S. M. (2009). Relationship between intraspecific variation in segment number and geographic distribution of *Himantarium gabrielis* (Linné, 1767) (Chilopoda: Geophilomorpha) in Southern Europe. *Soil Organisms, 81,* 359–371. Retrieved from http://www.senckenberg.de/files/content/forschung/publikationen/soilorganisms/volume_81_3/10_simaiakis.pdf

Timmerman, B. (2013). *Scolopendra gigantean*. Retrieved from http://bioweb.uwlax.edu/bio203/s2013/timmerma_benj

Chapter 6

Identity Thieves and Frauds

Arnold, C. (2013). Q&A: New spider weaves spider-shaped web. *National Geographic.* Retrieved from http://voices.nationalgeographic.com/2013/01/23/spider-decoy

Bradford, A. (2015). Corpse flower: Facts about the smelly plant. *LiveScience.* Retrieved from http://www.livescience.com/51947-corpse-flower-facts-about-the-smelly-plant.html

Flaherty, J. (2013). Raising the dead. *Tufts Now.* Retrieved from http://now.tufts.edu/articles/raising-dead

Florence, J. (2014). Mummy berry. *The Plant Health Instructor.* Retrieved from http://www.apsnet.org/edcenter/intropp/lessons/fungi/ascomycetes/Pages/MummyBerry.aspx

Frazer, J. (2015). Wonderful things: The amazing mimicry of the mummy berry fungus. *Scientific American.* Retrieved from http://blogs.scientificamerican.com/artful-amoeba/wonderful-things-the-amazing-mimicry-of-the-mummy-berry-fungus

Gould, S. E. (2014). Caterpillars use ants as butterfly babysitters. *Scientific American.* Retrieved from http://blogs.scientificamerican.com/lab-rat/caterpillars-use-ants-as-butterfly-babysitters

Lloyd, J. (1965). Aggressive mimicry in photuris: Firefly femmes fatales. *Science, 149,* 653–654. Retrieved from http://entomology.ifas.ufl.edu/baldwin/webbugs/3005_5006/Docs/firefly%20paper.pdf

Lloyd, J. (1980). Male photuris fireflies mimic sexual signals of their females' prey. *Science, 210,* 669–671.

Maculinea—The Large Blues. (2011). Retrieved from https://www.youtube.com/watch?v=e9jl2nC3X0U

Main, D. (2014). What I learned hunting decoy-weaving spiders in the Amazon. *Popular Science*. Retrieved from http://www.popsci.com/article/science/what-i-learned-hunting-amazonian-spiders-weave-fake-spiders

Marshall, M. (2016). Zoologger: The very hungry caterpillar usurps a queen. *New Scientist*. Retrieved from https://www.newscientist.com/article/dn18439-zoologger-the-very-hungry-caterpillar-usurps-a-queen

National Geographic. (2015). *What makes the corpse flower stink so bad?* Retrieved from http://news.nationalgeographic.com/2015/09/150930-stinky-corpse-flower-chicago-botanic-garden-blooms

Ngugi, H. K., & Scherm, H. (2006). Mimicry in plant-parasitic fungi. *FEMS Microbiology Letters, 257*, 171–176. Retrieved from http://femsle.oxfordjournals.org/content/femsle/257/2/171.full.pdf

Nguyen, T. C. (2007). Firefly's flash can bring sex or death. *LiveScience*. Retrieved from http://www.livescience.com/4640-firefly-flash-bring-sex-death.html

NPR. (2009). *Butterfly does great ant impressions.* Retrieved from http://www.npr.org/templates/story/story.php?storyId=100341264

Nuwer, R. (2012). Spider builds fake spider decoy. *Smithsonian Magazine*. Retrieved from http://www.smithsonianmag.com/smart-news/spider-builds-fake-spider-decoy-168663359

Pollak, T. (2015). *About that smell . . .* Retrieved from http://my.chicagobotanic.org/horticulture/behind-the-scenes/spike-update-about-that-smell

Segelken, R. (1997). Lured and liquidated, gullible male fireflies supply 'femmes fatales' with a lifesaving chemical. *Cornell Chronicle*. Retrieved from http://www.news.cornell.edu/stories/1997/09/cornell-biologists-report-mimicry-and-murder-night

University of California Botanical Garden at Berkeley. (2015). *Titan arum*. Retrieved from http://botanicalgarden.berkeley.edu/titan-arum

Wilton, P. (2009). Butterfly mimics 'talk' like ants. *Oxford Science Blog*. Retrieved from http://www.ox.ac.uk/news/science-blog/butterfly-mimics-talk-ants

Howler monkey

About the Authors

Jenn and Charlie are Boston-based science nerds who met through stand-up comedy. By day, Jenn writes science textbooks and Charlie slings data for a cancer research company. By night, they make comedy films and stay up past their bedtime e-mailing pictures of weird animals to each other.

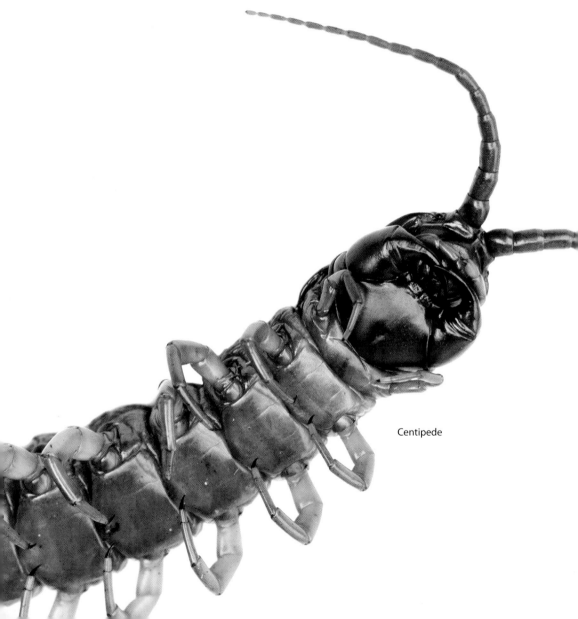

Centipede

Image Credits

The publisher would like to thank the following for their permission to reproduce their images:

Page 11: emotingsheep.wixsite.com; Page 14: Emmanuel Douzery; Page 22: DIAC images; Page 23: Allison Shaw/Department of Ecology and Evolutionary Biology; Page 25: camille meehan.com; Page 26: André Karwath; Page 27: Aaron Pomerantz/PeruNature.com; Page 41: Matthew Miller; Page 50: Kate/Flickr; Page 51: Flip De Nooyer/Minden Pictures (bottom); Page 56: Craig Mackay; Page 59: tested.com; Page 65: Rankin1958/WikiCommons (bottom); Page 66: Igor Siwanowicz; Page 68: Necrophorus/WikiCommons; Page 69: Alastair Rae; Page 71: Ian Redding; Page 77: Michael Rothbart/University of Wisconsin-Madison (top); Page 80: Lary Reeves; Page 84: Jade Florence; Page 85: Caleb Slemmons/National Ecological Observatory Network